Great Wall of China

BY ELIZABETH RAUM

RiverStream

RiverStream Illustrated
Great Reading • Real Learning

Amicus High Interest hardcover edition is an imprint of Amicus
P.O. Box 1329, Mankato, MN 56002
www.amicuspublishing.us

RiverStream Publishing reprinted with permission of
Amicus Publishing.

Library of Congress Cataloging-in-Publication Data
Raum, Elizabeth.
Great Wall of China / Elizabeth Raum.
     pages cm. — (Ancient wonders)
 Summary: "Describes the Great Wall of China, one of the
ancient wonders of the world, including how and why it was
built, the dynasties behind its construction, what it was used for,
and what it's like today" —Provided by publisher.
 Includes bibliographical references and index.
 ISBN 978-1-60753-467-9 (library binding : alk. paper) —
 ISBN 978-1-60753-682-6 (ebook)
 1. Great Wall of China (China)—Juvenile literature. I. Title.
 DS793.G67R38 2015
 951—dc23
                                                    2013028301

Editors   Kristina Ericksen and Rebecca Glaser
Series Designer   Kathleen Petelinsek
Book Designer   Heather Dreisbach
Photo Researcher   Kurtis Kinneman

Photo Credits
Alamy, 10, 13, 19, 24; Bridgeman Art Library, 23;
Corbis, 17, 28; Getty Images, 5, 14, 20; Shutterstock, cover, 6;
Superstock, 9, 26

 2 3 4 5   18 17 16
RiverStream Publishing
Printed in the United States
ISBN 978-1-62243-240-0 (paperback)

Table of Contents

The Longest Wall

The Great Wall of China is the longest wall in the world. It winds through China like a giant dragon. It has become a **symbol**, or sign, of the hard-working Chinese. After all, they began building it about 2,500 years ago. It took more than 2,000 years to finish!

The Great Wall winds through China.

The Great Wall is so long that it could stretch from Alaska to Texas.

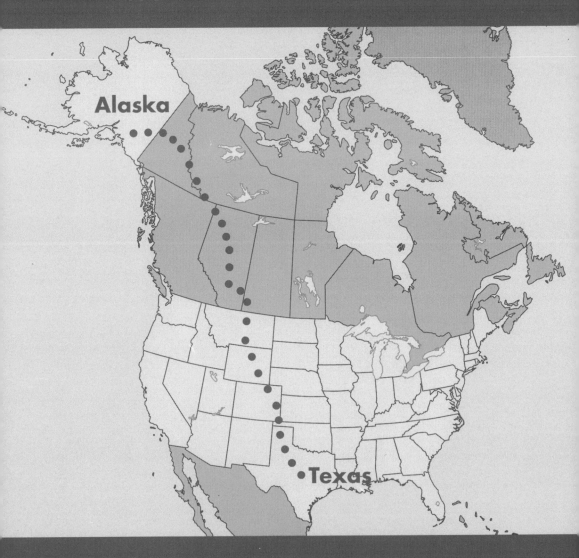

Alaska

•Texas

 Why don't we know the exact length?

The Chinese call the wall the "Long Wall of Ten Thousand Li." Ten thousand **li** is about 3,125 miles (5,029 km). No one knows the exact length of the wall. Many think it is about 4,000 miles (6,438 km) long. That's the distance from Alaska to Texas!

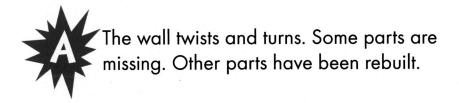

The wall twists and turns. Some parts are missing. Other parts have been rebuilt.

The wall is about 25 feet (8 m) tall. It is wide, too. Five people can ride horses side-by-side on top of the wall. Some thought it could be seen from the Moon. That's not true. No buildings on Earth are that big—not even China's great big wall.

Many people can walk side-by-side on the wall.

 How did Shi Huangdi (pictured above) become
the first emperor?

Who Built the Wall?

Long ago, rulers built walls for safety. In 221 **BC**, Shi Huangdi, of China's Qin **dynasty**, became China's first **emperor**. He wanted to keep enemies out. He built new walls. He linked them to old ones. This was the start of China's Great Wall.

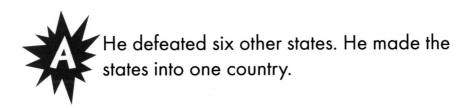 He defeated six other states. He made the states into one country.

Millions of people built the wall. Many were soldiers. The first emperor used 300,000 soldiers for it. Criminals worked on the wall, too. This was part of their punishment. Many people were forced to work on the wall. They had no choice and got no pay. Sometimes, even children had to help.

Thousands of workers were forced to help build the wall.

Each emperor had new
sections of wall built.

Shi Huangdi ruled for 15 years. Then a new family ruled. They also worked on the wall. Over the next 2,000 years, each new dynasty built parts of the wall. The Han, Sui, and Jin dynasties built major parts. The Ming dynasty finished the wall. They built it to last.

Building the Wall

The wall is made from many different materials. In deserts, workers used sand, **reeds**, and sticks. In other places, they used gravel, stone, or bricks. Sometimes they marked the path with wooden posts. They joined them with boards. Then they poured in stone and gravel. They packed it down. Finally, they laid bricks on top to make a path.

 How did workers carry bricks to the wall?

Stones were used to build many parts of the Great Wall. Some of them have fallen down.

 On their backs!

The wall builders followed the shape of the land. They used lakes or rivers as **natural borders**. The walls curved up steep mountains. On high ridges, the wall is shorter. The mountain helps keep enemies out. Gates let traders pass from one side to the other.

The wall curves around mountains, lakes, and rivers.

Soldiers kept a lookout from watchtowers.

Q Why did soldiers send smoke signals?

Workers also built watchtowers to help protect the border. They put a tower every 2 miles (3.2 km). The wall has more than 7,000 towers. Many are two or three stories tall. Soldiers watched from the towers. If they saw enemies, they sent up smoke signals.

 Soldiers nearby watched for signals. They came to help.

The Wall Crumbles

The Ming dynasty ended in 1644. The next rulers made peace with neighboring countries. They stopped repairing the wall. It began to crumble.

In the 1930s, China fought Japan. Some battles took place at the wall. Newspapers wrote about it. Artists drew it. The pictures made people around the world curious about the Great Wall.

**Battles between China and Japan
drew attention to the Great Wall.**

China did not welcome visitors. But, in 1972, U.S. President Richard Nixon went to China. It was a sign that China was changing. Tourists started visiting China.

At first, only a few people came. The number grew. Today about 10 million people visit China each year. Most see the Great Wall. It is China's biggest tourist site.

President Nixon and his wife visited the Great Wall in 1972.

In some places, the wall has crumbled or been damaged.

 Why do people damage the wall?

The Great Wall Today

Many visit the wall near Beijing. Beijing is China's capital. The wall here has been fixed. It is in good condition. That's not true for most of the wall. The Great Wall is falling down. Storms have damaged it. People take bricks and stones. Road crews smash holes in it to make new roads.

 Many do not realize its great history.

China began to protect the wall. In 2003, they made laws to stop the damage. People who harm the wall are fined. People cannot take bricks or stones from it. China is working to save the Great Wall. With hard work, it will last another 1,000 years.

Workers rebuild the eastern part of the wall.

Glossary

BC "Before Christ," signifying a year before the birth of Christ.

dynasty A series of rulers within a family.

emperor A ruler or king.

li A unit of measurement used in China equal to about 1,640 feet (500 m).

natural border A border between states or countries formed by mountains, rivers, lakes, or other land features.

reed A tall grass with hollow stems and broad leaves.

smoke signal A pattern of smoke puffs that form a message.

symbol Something that represents something else; a sign.

Read More

Challen, Paul C. *Hail! Ancient Chinese.* New York: Crabtree Pub., 2011.

Henzel, Cynthia Kennedy. *Great Wall of China.* Edina, Minn.: ABDO Pub. Co., 2011.

Riggs, Kate. *Great Wall of China.* Mankato, Minn.: Creative Education, 2009.

Websites

Geography for Kids: China capital, history, map, flag, and people.
http://www.ducksters.com/geography/country/china.php

The Great Wall—Ancient China for Kids
http://china.mrdonn.org/greatwall.html

The Great Wall of China
http://www.activityvillage.co.uk/the-great-wall-of-china

Index

About the Author

Elizabeth Raum has worked as a teacher, librarian, and writer. She has written dozens of books for young readers. She likes doing research and learning about new topics. After writing about ancient wonders, she wants to travel the world to visit them! To learn more, visit her website at www.elizabethraum.net.